Still Standing

90 Days of Wisdom for Moms of Addicts

Valerie Silveira

STILL STANDING

90 Days of Wisdom for Moms of Addicts

Published by The Still Standing Group

ISBN 978-0-9861104-3-6

Cover Illustration by Svetlana Dragicevic

Rich,

Thank you for choosing to be Jordan and Sean's dad. We started our lives together eighteen years ago, full of hopes and dreams. We could never have imagined where the road would lead; probably a good thing we didn't know. I do not fully understand the challenges a stepfather of an addict faces, but I do know it has not been easy. I am grateful every day that you have stuck by my side as a husband and as a father. We have traveled this path through many tears, and too many emotions to list, yet we have managed to come out stronger. Perhaps it was because we somehow found the laughter, among the tears. Together we can, and will, make it through anything - you and me babe. I love you.

Val

NOTE: The images reference a website and Facebook page that have been updated. Connect with Valerie here:

www.ValerieSilveira.com

www.Facebook.com/ValerieSilveira

ACTION #1: DECIDE TO STAND UP & FIGHT

ACTION #3: PUT ON YOUR OXYGEN MASK

ACTION #4: BUILD YOUR CIRCLE OF STRENGTH

ACTION #5: CHANGE YOUR ATTITUDE

ACTION #6: ADJUST YOUR FOCUS

ACTION #7: STOP BEING A CONTROL FREAK

ACTION #8: STAND <u>ON</u> YOUR STORY

ACTION #9: MAKE MEANING FROM THE MADNESS

Acknowledgements

Thank you to my friend Chris' dad Ron, from whom I received my first "motivational" speech around their kitchen table when I was eleven years old. To Gary, who introduced me to my first professional motivational speaker, Brian Tracy, in the early 90s. Little did I know how valuable these lessons would be, and how desperately I would need them many years later after all hell broke loose.

I am thankful to the dozens of other leaders and mentors who have influenced my life over the years.

I am grateful to my mom, Sandy Chiupka, who thinks I am a much better person than I am. You too have walked a very difficult path, "losing" your granddaughter, and knowing your daughter was going through hell, yet you are still standing. Your love and support mean the world to me.

To Svetlana Dragicevic, you continue to be a blessing, one for which I am eternally grateful. Your ability to extract a vision from my mind and onto paper is astounding. You have allowed a person who never thought of herself as artistic, to see her art come alive, and to the next level. Thank you.

Note to Moms of Addicts

You have ridden the Roller Coaster From Hell, much of the time feeling alone. I took that terrifying ride for thirteen years, never knowing what was up ahead in the darkness. Just as your daughter or son did not plan to be an addict, you certainly never thought you would be the mother of an addict. I sure did not, yet here we are. I wish that I had the magic answer, the blow that would knock your daughter or son's drug addiction Beast out for good. You know as well as I do that magic does not exist. There are combinations of things that can and do work for many addicts, but that is for the addict to figure out. If you had the ability to save your child, you would have done it long ago.

If you have read "Still Standing After All the Tears," you know my mission is to help you to battle your own Beast. As the mom of an addict, yours is the Codependent Enabler Beast, a two-headed monster that moved in with you, and over the years, has all but taken over your life.

I pray every day for your sons and daughters - that one day he or she will stand up and fight; they will stand victoriously over their Beasts. In the meantime, it is my heart's desire to help you, even in some small way to battle your own Beast. It is time you found joy, happiness, sense of peace, hope for the future, and your self-confidence. It is time to get back to the business of living your life.

You inspire me more than you will ever know, and I hope one day to meet you in person. The opportunity to guide you through the darkness is one that I do not take lightly. Life is going by at warp speed, so do not waste another moment of your precious time, lying down on the mat with your Beast on top of you. The time is now for you to Stand Up and Fight.

Honored to be standing with you,

Valerie

Following are updated pages to those noted in the images:
www.ValerieSilveira.com
www.Facebook.com/ValerieSilveiraAuthorSpeaker

When All Hell Broke Loose

(from "Still Standing After All the Tears")

In August 2004, my only daughter suffered a near-fatal gunshot wound, at the hands of her ex-boyfriend, a gang member.

Three years before the shooting, Jordan made her way from our safe, comfortable suburban life, into another world. We spent those three years leading up to the shooting, attempting to get her off her collision course. In the hospital, I stayed by Jordan's side nearly twenty-four hours a day. Laying in the dark one night in my makeshift bed pressed up against her hospital bed, my eighteen-year-old daughter asked, "Mommy, will you pray with me?"

She had never asked me to pray before, and frankly, I am not very comfortable praying out loud, but that night I held her hand and prayed my heart out. Afterward, it felt as if our nightmare would end, but it was far from over. I would need to put on my seatbelt and strap down my shoulder harness. My ride on the Roller Coaster From Hell was about to get a lot worse.

It would take a few years into the ride to confirm what I had suspected - Jordan was a drug addict. Today she is addicted to heroin.

As any mother would, I tried everything I knew in an attempt to save Jordan from her drug addiction Beast. I put on my Supermom Cape and came to her rescue repeatedly. My help never moved Jordan closer to battling her Beast, but I could not stop trying to save her. The further her life spiraled downward; the deeper mine spiraled into darkness.

My Beast is a two-headed monster. Not only was I an enabler, but my happiness and a sense of purpose had become dependent upon my daughter's willingness to battle her Beast. I was a codependent.

The best way I know how to describe nearly thirteen years of my life is that I was shoved, kicking and screaming onto a roller coaster with my Codependent Enabler Beast by my side. I rode it painfully up one hill and screaming down the next, trapped in a cycle of a mother's hope and suffocating disappointment. With every twist and turn, fear gripped me, and I held on for dear life.

The ride took me through health issues, a web of lies, financial stress, and a broken family. I rode through a world I never wanted to know, the legal system, failed rehabs for Jordan, a serious strain on my marriage, and constant emotional pain.

No matter what the consequences were to my health, finances, or marriage, I continued to strap on the Supermom Cape, choosing to believe the lies and accept the deceit. I covered my ears and eyes and tried to convince myself "this time it will be different." At the core of my actions were love and fear. I desperately wanted my baby back, and I was terrified of what might happen if I pulled out the safety net, if I took off the Cape.

It seemed *everybody else's kids* were doing well while I was living every mom's worst nightmare - losing a child, over and over again. My heart was shattered into a million pieces, standing helplessly as my precious daughter lost herself to drug addiction, despite how much I tried to help her. There was no closure and no way to heal. I was stuck. The world was turning without me, without Jordan, without us. With each failed attempt at saving her, I convinced myself I was a colossal failure as a mother; the part of me I valued most.

One day I asked myself the same question I had asked Jordan many times, "Where is your rock bottom?"

It was then that I realized a truth - if I had the ability to save Jordan from herself, from her Beast, I would have done it long ago. I had hit my rock bottom.

The Supermom Cape did not detach without pain, but I removed it; I stopped enabling Jordan. The codependency part of my Beast did not go down as easily. My heart ached for my daughter whose twenties were slipping into the past while she was lost in the belly of her Beast. I missed Jordan every second of every day.

Eventually, I began to accept that my best days were behind me. I was a victim who had been unfairly handed a "life sentence." I was at my lowest point, about to give up, when I made a decision that quite possibly saved my life. I decided to Stand Up and Battle My Beast.

~~~~~~~~~~

In *Still Standing After All the Tears: Putting Back the Pieces After All Hell Breaks Loose*, I share my very painful and personal journey that shattered my heart into a million pieces, and the actions I took to put those pieces back together and keep them together.

Still Standing: Wisdom for the Moms of Addicts provides more wisdom and insight to encourage you to stay in the battle, and to help you stand.

Update to Valerie's Story

On the morning of August 29, 2016, I got that knock on the door; the knock all moms of addicts fear.

I had done the work in this book, so my Beast was very much under control. He would occasionally knock on my door, but I had learned not to answer it. That morning, he didn't knock; he broke my door down – a home invasion.

A beautiful young woman around my daughter's age delivered the news - Jamie died the night before. Detectives arrived the next day to let us know she died from multiple gunshot wounds to the chest.

Yes, that dropped me to my knees. I rolled over onto my back, and my Beast got on top of me, in that comfortable place where he had been for so many years. This time I only stayed down for a short while. Although my heart was once again shattered, I am a much stronger and courageous woman. I have the peace that surpasses all understanding. It wasn't long before I decided to once again Stand Up and Fight. That is just what I have done.

Before her death, I referred to Jamie as "Jordan."

Introduction

Your child is an addict. One of mine is an addict too. It is the greatest disappointment and heartbreak of my life. I imagine it is the heartbreak of your life as well.

I wrote this book to speak specifically to moms of addicts, as a companion to *Still Standing After All the Tears: Putting Back the Pieces After All Hell Breaks Loose*, which guides anyone through a battle with a Beast. I encourage you to read that book. It is my story, but importantly it contains the Nine Actions to Battle Your Beast, in detail. As the mother of an addict, you will identify with the stories and perspectives in that book.

This book contains ninety quotes, inspired by *Still Standing After All the Tears*, providing you with one thought for each of the next ninety days. Each quote includes additional insight and perspective on the topic. The thoughts might be familiar to you if you have read my books, blogs, or follow me on social media.

Our children will live with (and hopefully battle) their drug addiction Beast for the rest of their lives. As a result, to one degree or another, we will deal with our Beasts for the remainder of ours. We are in this for the long haul. When it comes to something as serious as battling a Codependent Enabler Beast, you will need constant reminders, reinforcement, encouragement, and even a push now and again.

The Nine Actions to Battle Your Beast are powerful. They changed my life; one that I did not think would ever get better unless my daughter beat her drug addiction Beast. Work them into your life, and begin to live them every day. The more you do, the easier your battle becomes, and the less you will hear from your Beast.

Stay alert - your Codependent Enabler Beast will be continuously on the lookout for an opportunity to stick his foot back into the doorway of your life.

The Codependent Enabler Beast

Beasts come in all shapes and sizes. Some arrive because of an alcoholic or addict in the family, abuse, abandonment, an accident or illness, loss, perfectionism, or something else. Many are a combination of two or more. A Beast is a situation, person, attitude, or circumstance that has left you lost, defeated, frustrated, angry, hopeless and helpless, or living in paralyzing fear. Our Beasts remind us of the past, keep us from living in the present, and fearful of the future.

Moms of addicts live with the Codependent Enabler Beast, a two-headed monster that has you living in a constant state of hope and crushing disappointment.

This Beast will whisper in your ear or shout at the top of his lungs - convincing you of the lie - that your child's addiction is your fault. Over time, guilt begins to weigh heavily on you, and the shame

3

forces you to withdraw. Society adds a heaping portion of stigma, like a cherry on top of your shame and guilt pie. Shame, guilt, and stigma begin to suffocate you. Your heart has been shattered into a million pieces as you watch helplessly while your son or daughter becomes lost in the belly of their drug addiction Beast. Little by little, you begin to lose yourself, to lose hope of ever being happy again.

Your Codependent Enabler Beast has become a part of you, but it is NOT who you are. Somewhere deep down is the person you were before all hell broke loose. Inside of you is more courage, wisdom, and strength than you might imagine.

This Beast can be removed from your life. You can learn to be happy again, hopeful for the future, and to live with peace (most of the time), and it can be done no matter where your child is in their addiction. I know because I stood up to my Beast at my lowest point, during my darkest days, with my daughter still very lost. Many moms of addicts are using these actions to put the pieces back together. I hope that you will too.

Nine Actions to Battle Your Beast

At the time I stood up to fight, I could barely sit up. By the grace of God, responsibility to my son Sean, and support of my husband Rich, I found the last shred of my self-confidence and a tiny bit of hope. I fought hard to get even a small piece of "me" back. I stumbled many times, and I fell flat on my face. Each time I got back up determined to fight another day. Eventually, I was able to stand.

During that process, I discovered there were nine actions instrumental in my battle. These are the very actions I used to put the pieces of my shattered heart back together. They are what keep me standing. These actions are guiding other moms to live again.

Action #1: Decide to Stand Up and Fight

I mean really decide, don't just say it. Making the decision to Stand Up and Fight will be one of the best decisions you have ever made. When you get up off the mat, your Beast will not be happy. He will fight hard to bring you back down. As much as you have wanted your life to change for the better, life with your Beast has become your new "normal." Living in chaos, with fear and anxiety should not be your normal.

Decide that you will battle your Beast for as long as it takes. Be determined to stay in the fight no matter how long or how difficult, and that every time you are knocked down, you will get back up. It is a marathon, not a sprint.

Use these reminders to help you when you feel like giving up when you are losing hope of finding yourself, or when you feel as if it might be easier to stay down on the mat than to stand back up and fight again.

Action #2: Get On Your Spiritual Armor

Whatever spiritual beliefs you have, we can all agree that good and evil exist. There are so many differing beliefs that it would be impossible and irresponsible of me to attempt to include them all. I use what I know, and therefore, refer to the source of strength and all that is good, as God. The opposite of God is Satan, but I call him the Big Beast. If your beliefs differ from mine, you can still use the principles in this Action, modifying them for your personal spiritual beliefs.

Make no mistake about it - we are in not only a physical, emotional, and mental battle but also a spiritual one. When I was riding on the Roller Coaster From Hell, devastated, broken-hearted and confused - I tried to think my way through the minefield. Your spirit might feel as mine did so many times during my ride - lost, alone, and deflated. I was mad at God and frustrated with him, but do not make the mistake of believing you can think your way through this.

There is so much about addiction we don't understand. Most of life is beyond our control. The battle is too big for you alone, but it is not too big for God.

Action #3: Put On Your Oxygen Mask

This Action is all about self-care and love. Give yourself permission to be happy. You have heard flight attendants explain that in the event of a loss in cabin pressure, your oxygen mask will drop down. They instruct you to first, put it on your face before assisting others. Of course, the reason is that if you are without oxygen, you will pass out and be unable to help anyone.

Understandably, we moms find it nearly impossible to take care of ourselves while our children are self-destructing. It may help to remember that **you** are somebody's child too. You are as valuable as your child is, so treat yourself as the treasure that you are - one that needs care and nurturing, especially while battling a Beast.

Action #4: Build Your Circle of Strength

You may have begun to spend more time alone. No matter how much people care, unless they have lived it, they do not understand what life is like for the mother of an addict. Thankfully, for them, they have no idea what it takes you to make it through a day. You can still draw a tremendous amount of strength from your circle once you figure out where people fit into it.

The Circle of Strength represents the people in your life. When you learn more about it, you may be surprised where you thought people belonged, and where they probably should reside. Some

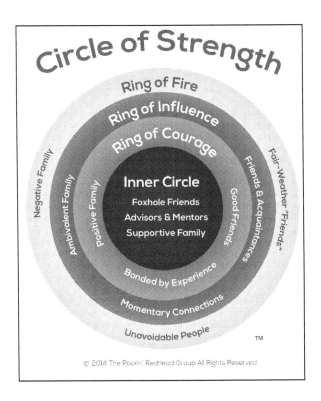

people, whom you would have automatically placed in your Inner Circle, may not belong there. Others you have in outer rings may just be those who should be in your Inner Circle. You will no

9

doubt be amazed at how much you can learn from those in your Ring of Fire if you choose to do so.

When you are feeling alone, or when the inevitable relationship disappointments occur, these messages will remind you how important it is to build and maintain your Circle of Strength. Build up the relationships that support you the most, and learn as much as you can from those that challenge you.

Action #5: Change Your Attitude

Attitude is a battle changer. You have lost your daughter or son repeatedly, so it is understandable if you don't feel like having a good attitude. Nobody would blame you for feeling as if life has handed you a lousy hand - it has.

The Beast wants and expects you to be negative, so knock him off balance with the right attitude.

Will having a negative attitude make your situation any better? Of course not! A good attitude will not change the grip your child's drug Beast has on them, but it will change the grip your Beast has on you.

Attitude is incredibly powerful, whether it is positive or negative. These quotes will help you when you spend too much time with Coulda, Shoulda, or Woulda, or you find yourself at another Pity Party. They will help you to recognize when you are becoming a Victim in Disguise or a Poor Me Victim.

Use them daily as a reminder that every single day, in every situation, no matter what happens – you have a choice concerning your attitude.

Action #6: Adjust Your Focus

What we focus on becomes magnified. When your son or daughter is out of control, your perspective will be out of focus.

Focus becomes a problem in two ways. First, you begin to focus on what others appear to have; that you have lost. With every milestone the children of your family and friends achieve, it reminds you of what you are missing. Before long, it appears that everyone but you has a perfect life. The fact is that some people do have easier lives than you do, but nobody has a perfect life.

Next, the more you fixate on your addicted child, the less you focus on other important relationships. If you have other children, they will suffer due to the imbalance of time, energy, attention, money, and concern you give your addicted child. Your marriage will likely suffer, along with many other relationships.

Without adjusting your Focus, you are in danger of becoming the Old Woman in the Cave (see the story of the Old Woman in the Cave in "Still Standing After All the Tears").

Action #7: Stop Being a Control Freak

This action is quite possibly the most challenging Action for moms of addicts. From the time you first held your child in your arms, you were convinced you could protect them, keep them safe, and teach them to make the right choices. Then all hell broke loose. The more out of control life with your daughter or son became, the more you attempted to control things – things for which you have no control.

Children come with Supermom Capes. Moms use them often as kids grow up, but they are seldom used more use than when their children are addicted. We strap on our Capes so often, eventually, we do not bother to take them off. We end up having them caught in doors, drawers, in our underwear and wrapped around our necks.

Removing the Cape is not easy under the best of circumstances. When your child is lost, it is nearly impossible, but necessary.

The Roller Coaster from Hell will take you on a ride through health issues, a web of lies, financial stress, broken relationships, and constant emotional pain. You can love the addict, but you are not required to stay on the ride.

If you could save your daughter, or your son, from their drug addiction Beast, you would not need this book. You would have saved them the first time you tried.

It is time to use the eight other actions to help you to Stop Being a Control Freak – to take off the Supermom Cape, and get on with living your life.

Action #8: Stand <u>On</u> Your Story

Be determined that you will become a better woman, not in spite of your story, but because of it. To a great extent, we are the sum of our experiences. Being the mom of an addict has changed you in ways you never imagined. Now you need to choose how the experience will influence the rest of your life. Resist the temptation to be stuck in the muck and mire of your incredibly sad and challenging journey.

Stand <u>ON</u> your story, not in it. Stand tall, and claim the reality of your life, but don't be taken down by it.

Although you are bruised, battered, and heartbroken, you can come out of this a more amazing person than you were before all hell broke loose. Allow the wisdom of this section to remind you of all that you are – much more than the mom of an addict.

Action #9: Make Meaning From the Madness

Although this is Action #9, do not think that it is something that you wait to begin working on, after the other eight are working together. What you are going through is huge, so you might have started to believe you have nothing to offer, not much to give.

Stepping outside of your story allows you to see the bigger picture and to connect with others who are struggling.

Do not wait until you have everything figured out, to begin with making meaning because that will likely be - never. You can make a difference right where you sit today. It does not have to be something earth shattering. You are in a unique position to make a difference for even one other person, even for just a moment. Remember, little things are big things.

Not only will this expand your world, but also the act of giving will most certainly come back to you many times over.

These reminders will inspire you to begin Making Meaning from the Madness that has become your life.

90 Days of Wisdom

Still Standing: 90 Days of Wisdom for Moms of Addicts is a follow-up book with quotes and encouragement inspired by *Still Standing After All the Tears: Putting Back the Pieces After All Hell Breaks Loose.*

It is easy to get off track with so much going on in your life. Although I expect your battle will become easier over time, it will always be a part of your life. As moms of addicts, we have a lifelong battle on our hands. You will need continuous reminders, inspiration, and encouragement. There will be times when you will need a hand up, to help you get back up off the mat.

Use the ninety quotes, words of wisdom and encouragement – one for each of the next ninety days, or simply choose one randomly.

The table of contents separates the quotes by each of the Nine Actions to Battle Your Beast. If you are struggling specifically with one of the Nine Actions, you can quickly find encouragement for that particular Action.

17

Keep the book with you, or download a copy, so you will have these words available when you need them most.

Following are full-color posters, presented in black and white, resulting in a variance in background shades. To see the posters in color, get the e-book version, which is readable on most portable devices.

Day One

BATTLE YOUR CODEPENDENT ENABLER BEAST

Parents of addicts live with a two-headed Beast. We keep trying to help our children, and wind up enabling them in their addiction. Your happiness and sense of purpose become dependent upon where your child is in their own battle. Love and fear keep you trapped in a cycle of hope and suffocating disappointment. It is time to stand up and battle <u>your</u> own Beast – the Codependent Enabler Beast.

- Valerie Silveira

www.AddictsFamily.com   Facebook: Addicts Family

It is natural that a certain amount of a mom's happiness and peace is dependent upon the well-being of their children. Moms of addicts are at an entirely different level- frantic to stop the drug addiction Beast. Since you cannot control that one, it is time for you to stand up & fight <u>your</u> Beast.

Day Two

ACTION #2: GET ON YOUR SPIRITUAL ARMOR

I have looked everywhere, but I still can't find my crystal ball! The truth is that nobody this side of heaven knows the future. Be sure to live today.

- *Valerie Silveira*

www.AddictsFamily.com   facebook.com/Addict's Family

You are desperate to know when your nightmare will end - how it will end. During most of my 13-year ride, I wanted to know what was up ahead on the road, but I could barely see what was right in front of me. Stop looking for a crystal ball; you will never find one. Rather than worry about the future, live for today.

Day Three

ACTION #3: PUT ON YOUR OXYGEN MASK

If you cannot put yourself at the top, at least get on the list!

- Valerie Silveira

www.AddictsFamily.com   facebook.com/Addict's Family

Mothers are cursed when it comes to putting ourselves before anyone, including the family dog. Moms of addicts continue to put their addicted children first, long into their adulthood. Remember that oxygen mask - if you pass out, you cannot help anyone. Eventually, get yourself to the top of the list.

Day Four

ACTION #4: BUILD YOUR CIRCLE OF STRENGTH

A foxhole friend is not just the person that you are in the foxhole with, but one that will go out on the battlefield and drag you back in. You know who your foxhole friends are, and they know who you are.

- *Valerie Silveira*

www.AddictsFamily.com   facebook.com/Addict's Family

If you are fortunate to have even one foxhole friend, treasure them - they are rare. We often have such a friend, but do not recognize their value while we are going through hell. Although it will be challenging to <u>be</u> a foxhole friend during your darkest days, doing just that will strengthen you for your battle.

Day Five

ACTION #5: CHANGE YOUR ATTITUDE

There are three people you should stay away from:

Mea Coulda,
Shirley Shoulda, &
I. Woulda.

- Valerie Silveira

www.AddictsFamily.com   facebook.com/Addict's Family

I spent so much time with coulda, shoulda, or woulda; they seemed like old friends, so I finally named them. You have no doubt spent countless hours beating yourself up over what you could have, should have, or would have done to prevent or stop your daughter or son's addiction. Stay away from these three!

Day Six

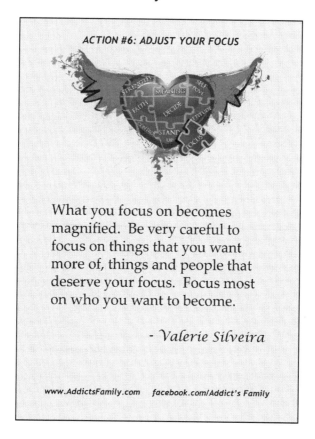

ACTION #6: ADJUST YOUR FOCUS

What you focus on becomes magnified. Be very careful to focus on things that you want more of, things and people that deserve your focus. Focus most on who you want to become.

- Valerie Silveira

www.AddictsFamily.com   facebook.com/Addict's Family

Currently, what you focus most of your time on is your lost child. You are still trying to battle for them, even when they are not. Be careful not to magnify the wrong things by focusing too much on what you cannot change, what has already happened, or what might happen. Focus more on the things you can control.

Day Seven

ACTION #7: STOP BEING A CONTROL FREAK

Start using the "F" word a lot more. Not that "F" word. I am talking about forgiveness. Forgive yourself, forgive others; you may even need to forgive your beast.

- Valerie Silveira

www.AddictsFamily.com   facebook.com/Addict's Family

Forgiveness can be difficult in many situations. When it comes to our children, we find it easier to forgive them for dragging us through hell, than to forgive ourselves, even for things that do not need forgiving. Start using the "F" word a lot more, and do not forget to use it on yourself.

Day Eight

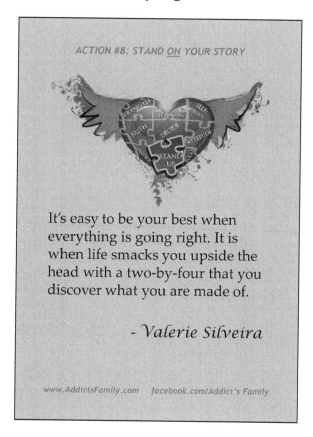

ACTION #8: STAND <u>ON</u> YOUR STORY

It's easy to be your best when everything is going right. It is when life smacks you upside the head with a two-by-four that you discover what you are made of.

- Valerie Silveira

www.AddictsFamily.com   facebook.com/Addict's Family

You envy people who appear to have everything going in the right direction. They seem happy and accomplished; living in peace. Remember, it is easy to be your best when everything is going right. Try being your best after all hell breaks loose – that is when you discover the incredible strength you have within.

Day Nine

ACTION #9: MAKE MEANING FROM THE MADNESS

Little things are big things. You don't have to be Mother Teresa to make a difference.

- *Valerie Silveira*

www.AddictsFamily.com   facebook.com/Addict's Family

We have the notion that we have to come up with something big to make a difference. A kind word of understanding spoken at the right moment could be earth shattering to someone who needed to hear those words. When it comes to making a difference, little things can be big things.

Day Ten

ACTION #1: DECIDE TO STAND UP & FIGHT

When you are down, the world is not going to stop turning. It is your responsibility to find a way to get back up.

- Valerie Silveira

www.AddictsFamily.com   Facebook: Addicts Family

You are stuck. The world seems to be spinning without you. You are down on the mat with your Beast on top of you, his claws around your throat while everybody else is moving on with their life. The fact is that life moves on with or without us. Do not wait for the world to pick you up – stand up!

Day Eleven

ACTION #2: GET ON YOUR SPIRITUAL ARMOR

Do not underestimate the Biggest Beast of all. He will work to separate you from God. Keep your spiritual armor on. You will need it for your battle.

- Valerie Silveira

www.AddictsFamily.com   facebook.com/Addict's Family

If there is a school of Beasts, Satan is the headmaster. I do not like to give him credit by using his name, so I call him the Big Beast. Both Beasts will work to separate you from God - your source of power, of all that is good. Keep your shield up and your armor on at all times.

Day Twelve

When your heart has been broken, you don't feel much like smiling, let alone laughing. It may seem as if you shouldn't laugh while your child is self-destructing. To get your joy back, you will have to make an effort. Make it a point to laugh every day. Laughter is the medicine you cannot afford to be without.

Day Thirteen

ACTION #4: BUILD YOUR CIRCLE OF STRENGTH

Sometimes water is thicker than blood.

- *Valerie Silveira*

www.AddictsFamily.com   facebook.com/Addict's Family

We tend to think that only family should be in our Inner Circle, especially during tumultuous times. Many of us do have supportive family members, but not everyone in your family will meet your expectations. Not all "family" is related by blood or marriage. Certain friends are closer than some family.

Day Fourteen

ACTION #5: CHANGE YOUR ATTITUDE

When I was a kid, my friend's dad told us, "...If you don't have the right attitude, you can't eat right, you can't sleep right, you can't poop right, you cant' do anything right." Ron was right – when you have a bad attitude, you can't do anything right.

www.AddictsFamily.com   Facebook: Addicts Family

This memory may seem silly. However, it is encouraging to know that a small thing we say can have a positive impact on other people's lives, and our own, for decades. You can be one of those people who inspire others with your great attitude, in spite of what you are facing.

Day Fifteen

ACTION #6: ADJUST YOUR FOCUS

When your nose is pressed up against the window of somebody else's life and it looks perfect, they probably haven't cleaned their windows in a while.

- Valerie Silveira

www.AddictsFamily.com   facebook.com/Addict's Family

Your world has been turned upside down, and it feels as if you are the only person going through trials. There are those that appear to have perfect lives but do not waste time focusing on another person's life or their journey. You have your hands full enough with your own.

Day Sixteen

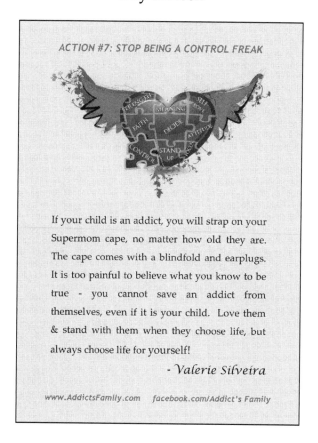

ACTION #7: STOP BEING A CONTROL FREAK

If your child is an addict, you will strap on your Supermom cape, no matter how old they are. The cape comes with a blindfold and earplugs. It is too painful to believe what you know to be true - you cannot save an addict from themselves, even if it is your child. Love them & stand with them when they choose life, but always choose life for yourself!

- Valerie Silveira

www.AddictsFamily.com   facebook.com/Addict's Family

One of the most painful truths you will face as the mother of an addict is that you are powerless to save your children from themselves, from their drug addiction Beast. You should never lose hope but come to terms with this reality. Just as you cannot choose life for them, nobody can choose it for you.

Day Seventeen

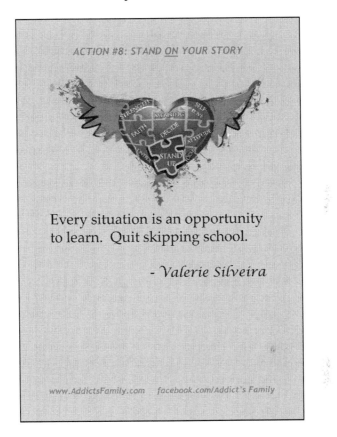

ACTION #8: STAND <u>ON</u> YOUR STORY

Every situation is an opportunity to learn. Quit skipping school.

- Valerie Silveira

www.AddictsFamily.com   facebook.com/Addict's Family

We try to avoid pain, so when a life lesson is beyond painful, we try to avoid it altogether. However, challenging situations are incredible opportunities to learn and grow. Life tends to throw you back into the class until you learn the lesson. Quit skipping school.

Day Eighteen

ACTION #9: MAKE MEANING FROM THE MADNESS

You only get one time around.

Make yours matter.

- *Valerie Silveira*

www.AddictsFamily.com   facebook.com/Addict's Family

Your time on this earth is brief, so you cannot afford to waste another day without making meaning. Think about these six words: you only get one time around. Do something meaningful with yours.

Day Nineteen

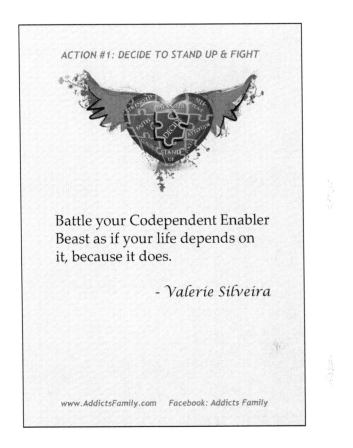

ACTION #1: DECIDE TO STAND UP & FIGHT

Battle your Codependent Enabler Beast as if your life depends on it, because it does.

- *Valerie Silveira*

www.AddictsFamily.com   Facebook: Addicts Family

Take this battle very seriously; it could mean the difference between living and actually living! When your Beast took over, a dark cloud settled over your heart, and you are simply going through the motions of living. Battle this thing as if your happiness, peace, and confidence depend on it because they do.

Day Twenty

ACTION #2: GET ON YOUR SPIRITUAL ARMOR

When you are on a mission from God, the Beast will be on his own mission. Do not let your guard down.

- Valerie Silveira

www.AddictsFamily.com   facebook.com/Addict's Family

No matter how strong you become, never let your guard down. The Beast is always looking for ways to separate you from God, to destroy your faith. Knowing God is your source of power, his job is to make you question your faith, and he is good at his job. Use your spiritual armor daily.

Day Twenty-One

ACTION #3: PUT ON YOUR OXYGEN MASK

Don't take responsibility for the actions of others. They need to learn their own lessons.

- *Valerie Silveira*

www.AddictsFamily.com   facebook.com/Addict's Family

Your child may be an adult, and yet you still feel a certain degree of responsibility for their actions. Yes, they have a disease, but they are responsible for treating the disease. Stop making excuses for them and worse yet, taking responsibility for their actions, or lack thereof. Focus on your lessons, your journey.

Day Twenty-Two

ACTION #4: BUILD YOUR CIRCLE OF STRENGTH

On those days when you don't have the strength to fight, it is okay to lay down. Let your circle fight for you. Then stand up again.

- *Valerie Silveira*

www.AddictsFamily.com   facebook.com/Addict's Family

Relationships include giving and receiving. During your battle, there will be times when you need to receive. There is nothing wrong with allowing your circle fight for you at times. Just do not stay down too long. Ultimately, you need to fight your battle.

Day Twenty-Three

ACTION #5: CHANGE YOUR ATTITUDE

Life isn't' fair; you can count on it. That is just the way it is. You have a choice to either become a victim, or to take the unfairness and turn it into opportunity. Which do you choose?

- *Valerie Silveira*

www.AddictsFamily.com   facebook.com/Addict's Famliy

When I get to heaven, I am going to ask God why life is so unfair. The thing is, when I get there, I won't care! Seriously, life is not fair. That is something you can count on. You have a choice to either become a victim or turn the unfairness into an opportunity. The choice is yours.

Day Twenty-Four

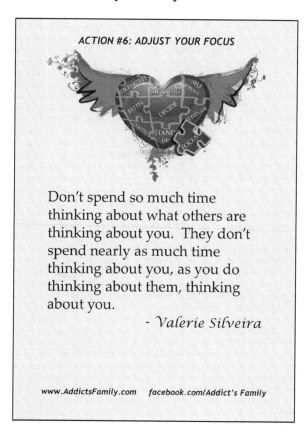

ACTION #6: ADJUST YOUR FOCUS

Don't spend so much time
thinking about what others are
thinking about you. They don't
spend nearly as much time
thinking about you, as you do
thinking about them, thinking
about you.

- *Valerie Silveira*

www.AddictsFamily.com   facebook.com/Addict's Family

Be assured that people are not spending as much time thinking

about you, as you might think. If you consider the amount of time,

you spend thinking about yourself and your problems, as

compared to every other person you have to think about, you will

realize how little people think about you.

Day Twenty-Five

ACTION #7: STOP BEING A CONTROL FREAK

If we had the ability to save our children from themselves, wouldn't it already be done?

- Valerie Silveira

www.AddictsFamily.com   facebook.com/Addict's Family

You have tried more times than you care to admit. If all it took were love, money, tears, bailing them out, yelling, or sleepless nights - you would have saved them a very long time ago. We must stop trying to fight their battle for them. Each person is responsible for fighting his or her battle.

Day Twenty-Six

ACTION #8: STAND <u>ON</u> YOUR STORY

Life experiences change us. It is up to us to decide what they will change us into.

- *Valerie Silveira*

www.AddictsFamily.com   Facebook: Addicts Family

You could easily stay down on the mat. It would not take much for you to give up, to accept that your best days are behind you. Do not allow yourself to become a bitter, sad, lonely, cynical woman. Stand up and become a better person because of your ride on the Roller Coaster from Hell.

Day Twenty-Seven

ACTION #9: MAKE MEANING FROM THE MADNESS

Consider the possibility that this is the moment for which you have been created.

- Valerie Silveira

www.AddictsFamily.com   facebook.com/Addict's Family

For the life of me, I could not come to grips with the fact that my daughter was lost in the belly of a drug Beast, and I was powerless to stop it. In the middle of the chaos, it never occurred to me that I could find a purpose in the darkness, yet I did. You too can are being prepared for something more.

Day Twenty-Eight

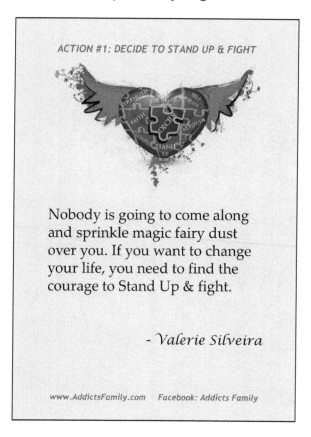

ACTION #1: DECIDE TO STAND UP & FIGHT

Nobody is going to come along
and sprinkle magic fairy dust
over you. If you want to change
your life, you need to find the
courage to Stand Up & fight.

- Valerie Silveira

www.AddictsFamily.com   Facebook: Addicts Family

We spend a great deal of time feeling sorry for ourselves as

parents of addicts, who could blame us? You sit for months, for

years, stuck - waiting for your son or daughter to change so your

life can change. The reality is that you have to find the courage to

Stand Up and Fight. It is in you; dig down deep and find it.

Day Twenty-Nine

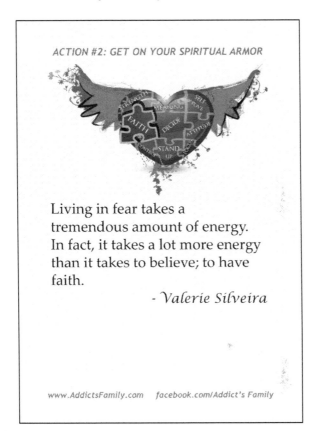

ACTION #2: GET ON YOUR SPIRITUAL ARMOR

Living in fear takes a tremendous amount of energy. In fact, it takes a lot more energy than it takes to believe; to have faith.

- *Valerie Silveira*

www.AddictsFamily.com   facebook.com/Addict's Family

We don't realize just how much energy we consume, living with worry and stress, which doesn't change anything for the better. Live in faith that you will receive enough - enough strength, courage, wisdom, support, peace, patience, and energy, sufficient for the battle. Enough to take down your Beast.

Day Thirty

ACTION #3: PUT ON YOUR OXYGEN MASK

If you spoke to others the way
you speak to yourself, you
wouldn't have many friends.

- Valerie Silveira

www.AddictsFamily.com   facebook.com/Addict's Family

You carry a tremendous amount of guilt, even though your son or daughter's addiction is not your fault. Guilt causes you to beat yourself up about everything. Before long, you are your worst enemy. Start speaking to yourself with words of love, encouragement, and support.

Day Thirty-One

ACTION #4: BUILD YOUR CIRCLE OF STRENGTH

When your heart is broken, there
is no plastic surgeon to heal your
wounds. There is something
better - Heart Glue. Turn to your
circle of strength; they are
holding your tubes of glue.

- Valerie Silveira

www.AddictsFamily.com   facebook.com/Addict's Family

I spent far too many years rejecting my heart glue, pretending I
did not need it. We feel alone as moms of addicts, so we isolate
ourselves from the world, compounding an already lonely path.
Be careful not to reject your heart glue.

Day Thirty-Two

ACTION #5: CHANGE YOUR ATTITUDE

When you find yourself saying, "why me" a lot, it may be time to ask, "why not me?"

- Valerie Silveira

www.AddictsFamily.com   facebook.com/Addict's Family

My daughter becoming a drug addict made no sense. I spent years in disbelief. Like me, you have probably asked a thousand times, "why me?" I don't know why this happened to you, or to me, but it does no good to continue asking. Instead, why not be the one who overcomes and inspires others?

Day Thirty-Three

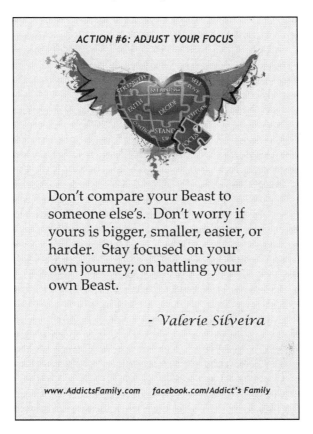

ACTION #6: ADJUST YOUR FOCUS

Don't compare your Beast to someone else's. Don't worry if yours is bigger, smaller, easier, or harder. Stay focused on your own journey; on battling your own Beast.

- *Valerie Silveira*

www.AddictsFamily.com   facebook.com/Addict's Family

We compare things. It is one way we gain perspective or attempt to make sense of a confusing situation. It becomes counterproductive when we focus too much on other people's lives or matters that do not concern us. Stay focused on your journey, on your battle.

51

Day Thirty-Four

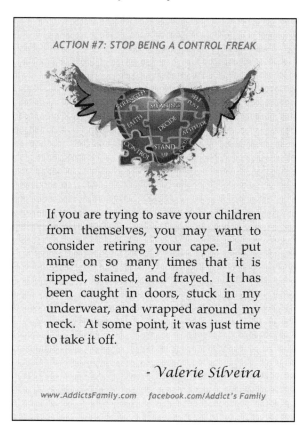

ACTION #7: STOP BEING A CONTROL FREAK

If you are trying to save your children from themselves, you may want to consider retiring your cape. I put mine on so many times that it is ripped, stained, and frayed. It has been caught in doors, stuck in my underwear, and wrapped around my neck. At some point, it was just time to take it off.

- Valerie Silveira

www.AddictsFamily.com   facebook.com/Addict's Family

Before you retire your Cape, remember that you had nothing but good intentions when you first put it on. Every time you wore it, you believed you could make a difference. There were times you were *certain* you could save your child from their drug Beast, but now it is time to untie the knot, to remove your Supermom Cape.

Day Thirty-Five

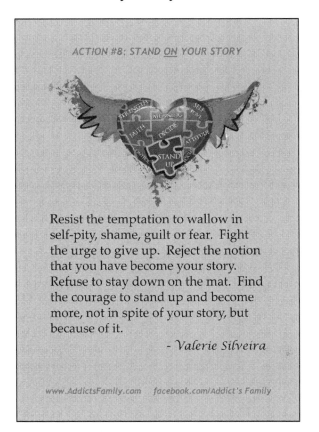

ACTION #8: STAND ON YOUR STORY

Resist the temptation to wallow in self-pity, shame, guilt or fear. Fight the urge to give up. Reject the notion that you have become your story. Refuse to stay down on the mat. Find the courage to stand up and become more, not in spite of your story, but because of it.

- Valerie Silveira

www.AddictsFamily.com   facebook.com/Addict's Family

It may be the path of least resistance to spiral down into the pit of despair. If you are already there, it is time to stand up. Refuse to remain a victim. Know that your best days are not behind you. Rise from the mat, and become all that you were born to be.

Day Thirty-Six

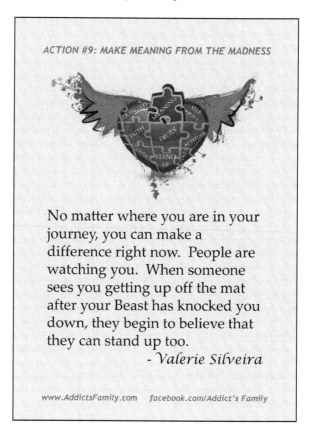

ACTION #9: MAKE MEANING FROM THE MADNESS

No matter where you are in your journey, you can make a difference right now. People are watching you. When someone sees you getting up off the mat after your Beast has knocked you down, they begin to believe that they can stand up too.

- *Valerie Silveira*

www.AddictsFamily.com   facebook.com/Addict's Family

If anyone has ever told you how much he or she admires you, looks up to you, or is inspired by you, then you know how great that feels. You might believe this only happens to people who have it all together, but that is not true. When people see you stand up and fight, it will give them hope.

Day Thirty-Seven

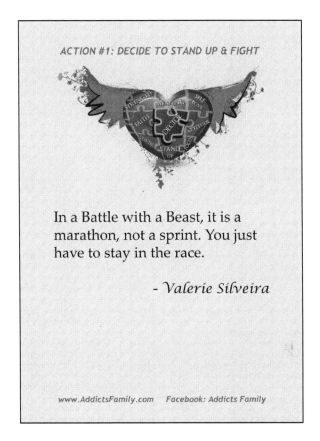

ACTION #1: DECIDE TO STAND UP & FIGHT

In a Battle with a Beast, it is a marathon, not a sprint. You just have to stay in the race.

- Valerie Silveira

www.AddictsFamily.com   Facebook: Addicts Family

There will be setbacks in the battle. Some days it will feel like two steps forward and one step back. On other days, it will feel more like one step backward and no steps forward. It took years for your Beast to control you; it will take a little time for you to reclaim your life. Stay in the race.

Day Thirty-Eight

ACTION #2: GET ON YOUR SPIRITUAL ARMOR

Be on your guard when fear creeps in; it is not from God. It is one of the battle tactics the Big Beast uses to separate you from God.

- Valerie Silveira

www.AddictsFamily.com   facebook.com/Addict's Family

God wants us to live in peace, not in fear. You need to move past exhausting fear to empowering faith. Fear is the opposite of faith, and you cannot have both at the same time. Choose faith over fear.

Day Thirty-Nine

ACTION #3: PUT ON YOUR OXYGEN MASK

Find out who is wearing your oxygen mask, and get it back.

- Valerie Silveira

www.AddictsFamily.com   facebook.com/Addict's Family

As the mom of an addict, you know who is wearing your oxygen mask. The question is whether you are willing to go and get it back.

Day Forty

ACTION #4: BUILD YOUR CIRCLE OF STRENGTH

When you are battling a Beast, you will find out who your true friends are.

- Valerie Silveira

www.AddictsFamily.com   facebook.com/Addict's Family

Inevitably, you will be disappointed by some of your relationships and pleasantly surprised by others. Rather than becoming cynical, victimized, or disappointed, consider it a learning experience. It is an opportunity to build some of your relationships even stronger, to let go of those holding you back, and to forge new ones.

Day Forty-One

We keep waiting for things to change, things for which we do not have control. Tomorrow, things will change with your son. Perhaps next week, your daughter will get clean. Maybe next year, your life will get back to "normal." TODAY is the only day you are guaranteed. Make TODAY count.

Day Forty-Two

ACTION #6: ADJUST YOUR FOCUS

WARNING: Lives lived out on social media may appear better than they really are.

- *Valerie Silveira*

www.AddictsFamily.com   facebook.com/Addict's Family

If you spend any amount of time on social media, you will need to adjust your focus constantly. Nobody's kids are perfect. Not one person is happy 24/7. Focusing on other people's lives may help you forget about yours temporarily, but it will delay your battle and your victory.

Day Forty-Three

ACTION #7: STOP BEING A CONTROL FREAK

Nobody knows what is around the next corner. Live for today!

- Valerie Silveira

www.AddictsFamily.com   facebook.com/Addict's Family

We hear it all the time - live for today. It is okay to think about the past and be concerned with the future, but with all of the past and future noise in our minds; it is no wonder we do not stay in the present. The bottom line is that nobody knows what is around the next corner, so it is foolish not to live for today.

Day Forty-Four

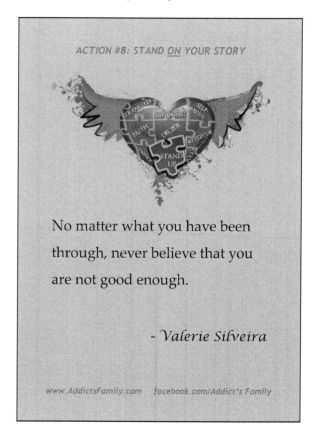

ACTION #8: STAND <u>ON</u> YOUR STORY

No matter what you have been
through, never believe that you
are not good enough.

- Valerie Silveira

www.AddictsFamily.com   facebook.com/Addict's Family

Many people have grown up in or lived through tremendous
hardship, heartbreak, and adversity, and yet managed not only to
survive but also to make something meaningful out of their lives.
Believe that YOU are good enough, not only to get through this
but also to make the rest of your life meaningful.

Day Forty-Five

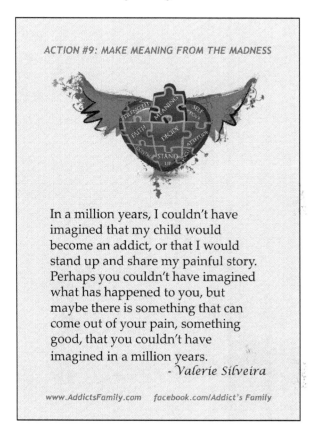

ACTION #9: MAKE MEANING FROM THE MADNESS

In a million years, I couldn't have imagined that my child would become an addict, or that I would stand up and share my painful story. Perhaps you couldn't have imagined what has happened to you, but maybe there is something that can come out of your pain, something good, that you couldn't have imagined in a million years.
- *Valerie Silveira*

www.AddictsFamily.com   facebook.com/Addict's Family

Something good can come out of all of this. You might not see it now, but your life can change completely in the coming months and years. It is up to you take action so that something meaningful will come out of your pain.

Day Forty-Six

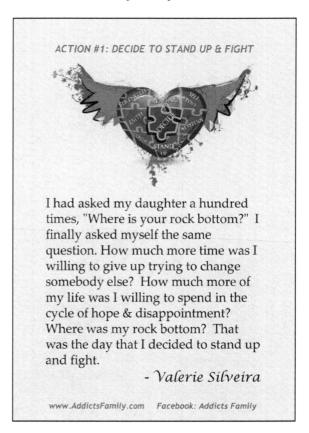

ACTION #1: DECIDE TO STAND UP & FIGHT

I had asked my daughter a hundred times, "Where is your rock bottom?" I finally asked myself the same question. How much more time was I willing to give up trying to change somebody else? How much more of my life was I willing to spend in the cycle of hope & disappointment? Where was my rock bottom? That was the day that I decided to stand up and fight.

- *Valerie Silveira*

www.AddictsFamily.com   Facebook: Addicts Family

I thought Jordan's shooting would be her rock bottom, but it was far from it. You cannot control another person's rock bottom, but you can control yours. Where is your rock bottom? Is today the day you finally Decide to Stand Up and Fight. Better yet, do not wait for rock bottom.

Day Forty-Seven

ACTION #2: GET ON YOUR SPIRITUAL ARMOR

The world will tell you that you have no right to feel peace in the midst of your own storm. Do not listen to the world. Your Codependent Enabler Beast will try to convince you that as a parent, you have no right to be at peace when your child is headed for disaster. He will tempt you to live with anxiety and fear. Do not listen. You have every right to be at peace, no matter what is going on around you.

- *Valerie Silveira*

www.AddictsFamily.com   facebook.com/Addict's Family

I understand firsthand, how difficult it is to get to a place of peace while your son or daughter is on a self-destructive path. Living in chaos, I was beyond exhausted. You are no doubt tired of living with anxiety every moment of every day. Do what I did, and go on a "frantic" quest for peace.

Day Forty-Eight

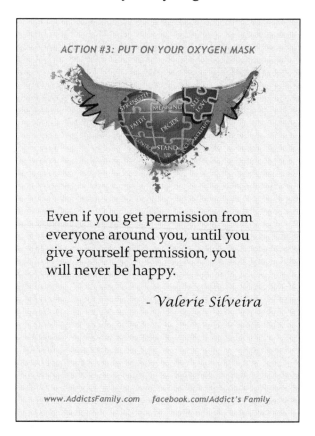

ACTION #3: PUT ON YOUR OXYGEN MASK

Even if you get permission from everyone around you, until you give yourself permission, you will never be happy.

- Valerie Silveira

www.AddictsFamily.com   facebook.com/Addict's Family

We have an easier time giving others permission to be happy than ourselves. Why don't you think you deserve to be happy? Is being miserable going to change the situation with your son or daughter? For you to be happy, you must give yourself permission.

Day Forty-Nine

ACTION #4: BUILD YOUR CIRCLE OF STRENGTH

When your battle is won, the people that you expected to be standing with you, may not be there. You may be bloodied & scarred, but you will be standing! And you will not be alone. When you look to your right and to your left, there will be a row of people standing shoulder to shoulder with you. Some of them you do not even know right now.

- *Valerie Silveira*

www.AddictsFamily.com   facebook.com/Addict's Family

We set expectations for ourselves and others. Often, we are let down by those we thought would battle with us, or stand in support of us. Trust that the right people will show up at the right times. You are not alone; as moms of addicts, we are in this together.

Day Fifty

ACTION #5: CHANGE YOUR ATTITUDE

Negativity is contagious. Make sure you are not infected.

- Valerie Silveira

www.AddictsFamily.com   facebook.com/Addict's Family

Negativity is very contagious. Even if you start out positive, it does not take much negativity to blow up a positive attitude. You have to fight hard to become a positive person, and even more so to remain one. Negativity is a contagion that is hard to eradicate. The cure is a positive attitude.

Day Fifty-One

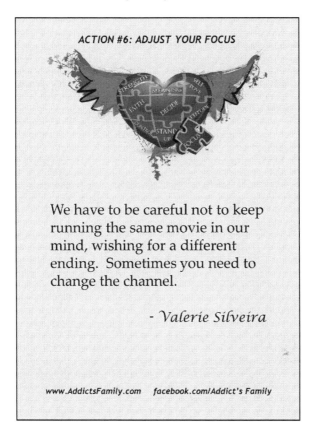

ACTION #6: ADJUST YOUR FOCUS

We have to be careful not to keep running the same movie in our mind, wishing for a different ending. Sometimes you need to change the channel.

- *Valerie Silveira*

www.AddictsFamily.com   facebook.com/Addict's Family

Stop beating yourself up. Quit running the scenes repeatedly in your head - every heartbreaking detail. It will not change what has happened and will prevent you from focusing on the now, on getting your life back. It is time to change the channel.

Day Fifty-Two

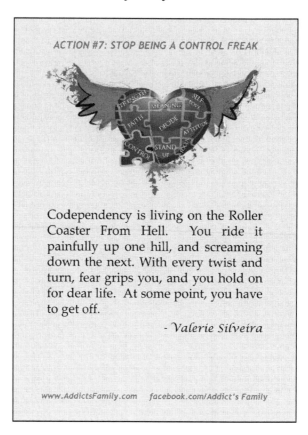

ACTION #7: STOP BEING A CONTROL FREAK

Codependency is living on the Roller Coaster From Hell. You ride it painfully up one hill, and screaming down the next. With every twist and turn, fear grips you, and you hold on for dear life. At some point, you have to get off.

- *Valerie Silveira*

www.AddictsFamily.com   facebook.com/Addict's Family

Your happiness has become dependent upon an addict. Although you did not ask to get on the ride, you can decide whether you will stay on it. You are not required to ride the Roller Coaster From Hell just because your child bought you the ticket.

Day Fifty-Three

BATTLE YOUR CODEPENDENT ENABLER BEAST

The most valuable lessons you will ever learn will come through your trials. One of your life's best teachers may be your Codependent Enabler Beast.

- Valerie Silveira

www.AddictsFamily.com   facebook.com/Addict's Family

It would be nice if we could learn from the mistakes or misfortunes of others, or better yet from life when it is all smooth sailing, but it does not work that way. You may not see it now, but trust that you are learning some of the most valuable lessons you will ever learn, just where you are.

Day Fifty-Four

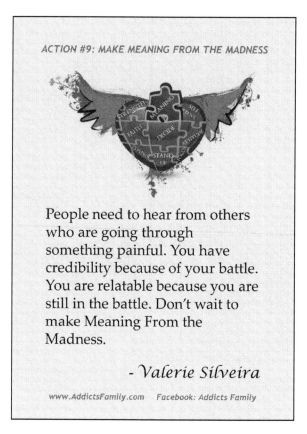

ACTION #9: MAKE MEANING FROM THE MADNESS

People need to hear from others who are going through something painful. You have credibility because of your battle. You are relatable because you are still in the battle. Don't wait to make Meaning From the Madness.

- Valerie Silveira

www.AddictsFamily.com   Facebook: Addicts Family

There is no reason that you cannot reach out to one-person right smack in the middle of your battle. People need to hear from real people like you, who understand, who are in the fight. Not only can you do this but you *should* do this. It will not only help others, but it will strengthen you for the fight.

Day Fifty-Five

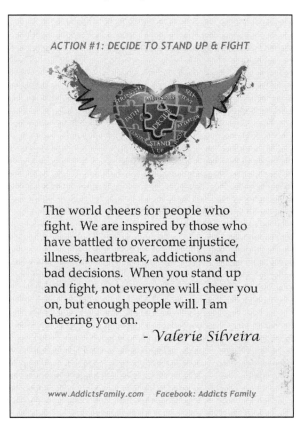

ACTION #1: DECIDE TO STAND UP & FIGHT

The world cheers for people who fight. We are inspired by those who have battled to overcome injustice, illness, heartbreak, addictions and bad decisions. When you stand up and fight, not everyone will cheer you on, but enough people will. I am cheering you on.

- Valerie Silveira

www.AddictsFamily.com   Facebook: Addicts Family

Many people are fascinated, even in awe of, celebrities, but the world cheers for people who have fought to overcome incredible obstacles. Those people inspire us. They empower, encourage, and motivate us. You can be one of these people.

Day Fifty-Six

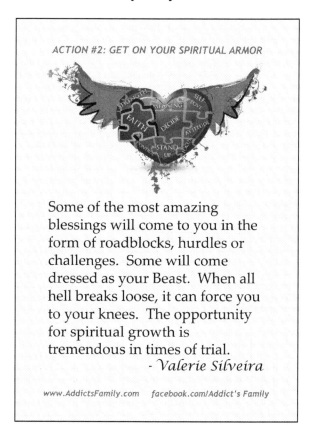

ACTION #2: GET ON YOUR SPIRITUAL ARMOR

Some of the most amazing blessings will come to you in the form of roadblocks, hurdles or challenges. Some will come dressed as your Beast. When all hell breaks loose, it can force you to your knees. The opportunity for spiritual growth is tremendous in times of trial.

- *Valerie Silveira*

www.AddictsFamily.com   facebook.com/Addict's Family

Your faith has been tested - repeatedly. Mine too. There were times when I dropped to my knees, calling out to God in despair, only to hear nothing. I continued to seek God, mainly because I did not know what else to do. I learned the teacher is often silent while the student is taking a test. Do not give up on God.

Day Fifty-Seven

ACTION #3: PUT ON YOUR OXYGEN MASK

You are stronger than you think.

- Valerie Silveira

www.AddictsFamily.com   facebook.com/Addict's Family

For years when my kids were small, I would voice that if anything ever happened to them, I would be "done." There were many times over a thirteen year period when I thought I might be done, but I found out I was much stronger than I realized. You are much stronger than you might think.

Day Fifty-Eight

ACTION #4: BUILD YOUR CIRCLE OF STRENGTH

Don't step onto the battlefield alone. Take some friends with you.

- *Valerie Silveira*

www.AddictsFamily.com   facebook.com/Addict's Family

As alone as you feel, do not make the mistake of becoming lonely. It is important that you take some people with you into the battle. It is mainly yours to fight, but not completely alone. You need the strength, courage, and support of other people.

Day Fifty-Nine

ACTION #5: CHANGE YOUR ATTITUDE

If you find yourself at a Pity Party, find the nearest exit. It won't be easy. In contrast to the warm welcome, few people will help you locate the exit door. Once you find it, run for the door and don't look back. Better yet, decline the invitation.

- *Valerie Silveira*

www.AddictsFamily.com   facebook.com/Addict's Family

How many Pity Parties have you attended while living with your Beast? I attended many. Some were private parties, but I attended just the same. Acknowledge your sadness and allow yourself some compassion. Just be careful, because it is nearly impossible to fight while in attendance at a Pity Party.

Day Sixty

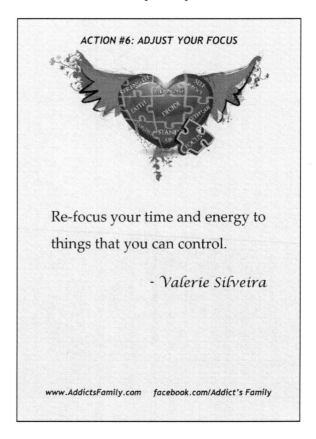

ACTION #6: ADJUST YOUR FOCUS

Re-focus your time and energy to
things that you can control.

- Valerie Silveira

www.AddictsFamily.com   facebook.com/Addict's Family

We spend far too much time focused on people and situations that
we cannot control. Stop spinning your wheels and learn to adjust
your focus to things that you can control. This type of adjustment
is not a one-time event. It will be a continuous process of re-
adjusting when your perspective and attitude are out of focus.

Day Sixty-One

ACTION #7: STOP BEING A CONTROL FREAK

There is a big difference between love strings and Supermom cape strings. You can cut the cape strings, but the love strings are un-severable. Putting away your cape does not mean you love your children any less.

- Valerie Silveira

www.AddictsFamily.com   facebook.com/Addict's Family

It is hard to take off the Supermom Cape for many reasons. One of them is that you confuse cape strings with love strings. You can cut cape strings, but love strings are un-severable. Continuing to live in insanity does not prove you love your son or daughter more, and taking off your cape does not mean you love them less.

Day Sixty-Two

ACTION #8: STAND <u>ON</u> YOUR STORY

Society makes sure parents of addicts have a steady stream of shame and guilt, adding stigma, like a cherry on top of our shame and guilt pie. We pile enough shame and guilt on ourselves as parents without anyone adding to it.

- *Valerie Silveira*

www.AddictsFamily.com   facebook.com/Addict's Family

Do not buy into society's stigma of you as the mom of an addict. The fact your child is an addict does NOT mean you are a terrible mother. You have piled enough undue shame and guilt on yourself over this; there is no need for you to allow outside influences to make things harder on yourself.

Day Sixty-Three

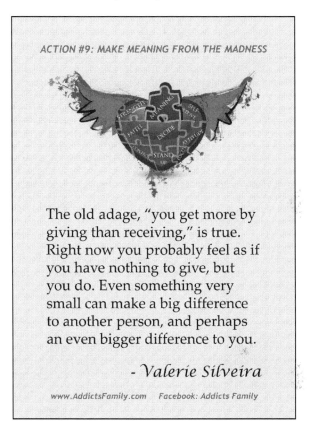

ACTION #9: MAKE MEANING FROM THE MADNESS

The old adage, "you get more by giving than receiving," is true. Right now you probably feel as if you have nothing to give, but you do. Even something very small can make a big difference to another person, and perhaps an even bigger difference to you.

- *Valerie Silveira*

www.AddictsFamily.com   Facebook: Addicts Family

I challenge you to take a step forward and make a tiny bit of meaning for someone else. If you do it with no expectation of anything in return, I can almost guarantee you will receive more by your genuine act of kindness than you gave. Go ahead and try it.

Day Sixty-Four

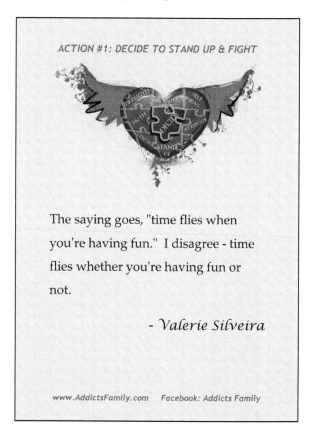

ACTION #1: DECIDE TO STAND UP & FIGHT

The saying goes, "time flies when you're having fun." I disagree - time flies whether you're having fun or not.

- *Valerie Silveira*

www.AddictsFamily.com   Facebook: Addicts Family

Every second that goes by, every moment we waste, every day we allow the Beast to control our lives, is the time we cannot recover. How much more of your precious time, are you willing to give up, feeling lost and defeated? Time is flying, so make the most of every minute of every day.

Day Sixty-Five

ACTION #2: GET ON YOUR SPIRITUAL ARMOR

Beasts are tough, but God is tougher.

- *Valerie Silveira*

www.AddictsFamily.com   Facebook: Addicts Family

This simple thought will help you in the darkest hours of your battle. When it felt as if I could not put one foot in front of the other, because the Beast was too strong, I would remind myself of this fact. Although Beasts certainly are tough, God is tougher.

Day Sixty-Six

ACTION #3: PUT ON YOUR OXYGEN MASK

Pre-flight instructions are pretty clear - put the oxygen mask on your own face before assisting others. If you live with a Codependent Enabler Beast, then you need to hear the instructions again. Put the oxygen mask on your own face before trying to assist others around you.

- *Valerie Silveira*

www.AddictsFamily.com   facebook.com/Addict's Family

While we, as moms, are running around trying to save our children from themselves, we forget to put the oxygen mask on our faces. We fear that taking care of ourselves is somehow selfish, but taking care of you gives you strength to care for others. Taking care of you <u>is</u> taking care of others.

Day Sixty-Seven

ACTION #4: BUILD YOUR CIRCLE OF STRENGTH

Newsflash – not all family members will support you in your battle. Don't put too much pressure on them. Some are simply negative, and others are living with their own Beast.

- *Valerie Silveira*

www.AddictsFamily.com   facebook.com/Addicts Family

A negative family member, who is non-supportive, is not surprising. However, when a person you expected to be supportive is not, it can be devastating. Do not be too hard on unsupportive family members, because many of them are living with their own Beasts, even if they do not realize it.

85

Day Sixty-Eight

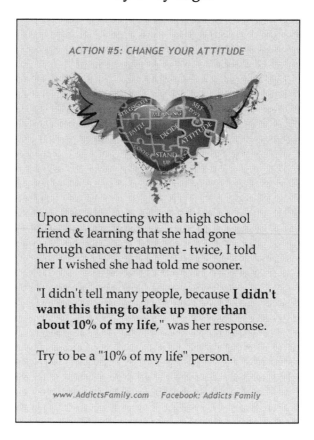

ACTION #5: CHANGE YOUR ATTITUDE

Upon reconnecting with a high school friend & learning that she had gone through cancer treatment - twice, I told her I wished she had told me sooner.

"I didn't tell many people, because **I didn't want this thing to take up more than about 10% of my life**," was her response.

Try to be a "10% of my life" person.

www.AddictsFamily.com   Facebook: Addicts Family

No doubt, your nightmare is taking up much more than 10% of your life. There were times when mine took up 90% of my life. Imagine what your life could be like right now if you only allowed your Beast to take up 10% of your life, or even 50%!

Day Sixty-Nine

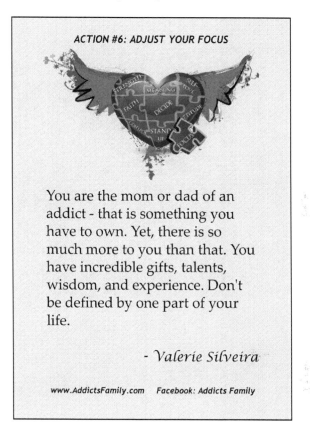

ACTION #6: ADJUST YOUR FOCUS

You are the mom or dad of an addict - that is something you have to own. Yet, there is so much more to you than that. You have incredible gifts, talents, wisdom, and experience. Don't be defined by one part of your life.

- Valerie Silveira

www.AddictsFamily.com   Facebook: Addicts Family

I felt different from other moms; I still do. We <u>are</u> different from mothers whose children are not addicted. I finally began to accept the difference, without allowing it to make me feel inferior. Refuse to allow yourself to be defined solely as the mom of an addict. You are so much more.

Day Seventy

ACTION #7: STOP BEING A CONTROL FREAK

The most painful truth that a parent of an addict, and especially a mother, will face is - that we are powerless to save our children from themselves. So, we stand at a crossroads with only 2 choices - either spiral into darkness, or stand up and fight. Parents of addicts - choose life!

- *Valerie Silveira*

www.AddictsFamily.com   facebook.com/Addict's Family

What good does it do for you to go down with your addict? How will it help anyone, including your child for you to spiral into darkness? Your sons and daughters have choices - they can choose to stand up and fight. You too have choices.

Day Seventy-One

ACTION #8: STAND <u>ON</u> YOUR STORY

As parents of addicts, we live in a world of shame, guilt, and stigma. It is time for us to come out of the shadows. It is time to stand on our stories, to shed the shame and guilt. It is time to remove the stigma.

- Valerie Silveira

www.AddictsFamily.com   facebook.com/Addict's Family

Stigma surrounds addicts and parents of drug abusers. Contrary to what society might believe, we are not walking around with needles sticking out of our arms. Stop hiding in the shadows, alone, ashamed, full of guilt, and pain. It is time for you to stand <u>on</u> your story, not in it.

Day Seventy-Two

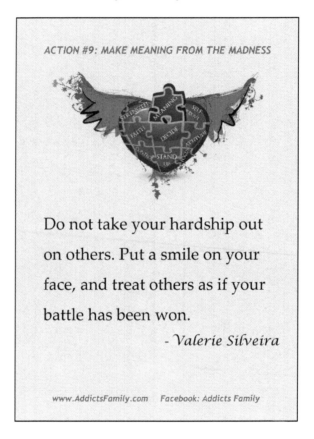

ACTION #9: MAKE MEANING FROM THE MADNESS

Do not take your hardship out on others. Put a smile on your face, and treat others as if your battle has been won.

- *Valerie Silveira*

www.AddictsFamily.com   Facebook: Addicts Family

Be careful not to take your hardship out on others. Do not be the person at the checkout counter who makes everyone else miserable, because you are going through a very hard time. Perhaps the checker is going through something worse.

Day Seventy-Three

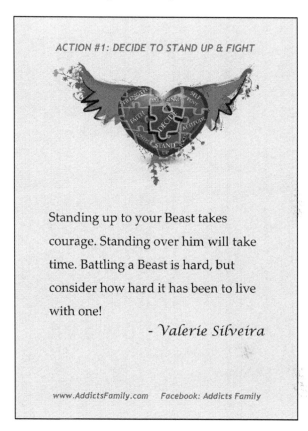

ACTION #1: DECIDE TO STAND UP & FIGHT

Standing up to your Beast takes courage. Standing over him will take time. Battling a Beast is hard, but consider how hard it has been to live with one!

- *Valerie Silveira*

www.AddictsFamily.com   Facebook: Addicts Family

Jordan's excuse for not standing up to fight is that it's "too hard." I am sure battling drug addiction is enormous, but what is her choice? What is your choice? Standing up to your Beast will take courage, and standing over him will take time. It will be hard to battle your Beast, but no more difficult than living with him.

Day Seventy-Four

ACTION #2: GET ON YOUR SPIRITUAL ARMOR

It is easy to be thankful when everything is going well. How thankful are you when all hell breaks loose? If you can't find something to be thankful for, you are not looking very hard.

- *Valerie Silveira*

www.AddictsFamily.com   Facebook: Addicts Family

When all hell breaks loose, your faith is tested - this is when you begin to understand that not all blessings come in the ways you might expect. Sometimes it is a blessing just to make it through an entire week without losing it. Every day you have the gift of life, is a day to be thankful.

Day Seventy-Five

ACTION #3: PUT ON YOUR OXYGEN MASK

Go outside and play.

- *Valerie Silveira*

www.AddictsFamily.com   Facebook: Addicts Family

There is something very healing about the outdoors. When the mind is too active, stressed, a walk can do wonders. Do you spend enough time outdoors? Go for a walk; take a hike, sit by a lake or river. Like your mom used to tell you - go outside and play!

Day Seventy-Six

ACTION #4: BUILD YOUR CIRCLE OF STRENGTH

The people in your Ring of
Fire can actually help you.
Negative or cynical people
act as a mirror. If you don't
like what you see when you
look into the Ring of Fire, be
careful you don't see yourself
in its reflection.

- Valerie Silveira

www.AddictsFamily.com   facebook.com/Addicts Family

The outer ring of the Circle of Strength is your Ring of Fire. It represents people who are challenging. Some are those people you are "stuck" with. If you cannot avoid certain people, take the opportunity to learn and grow from people in the Ring of Fire.

Day Seventy-Seven

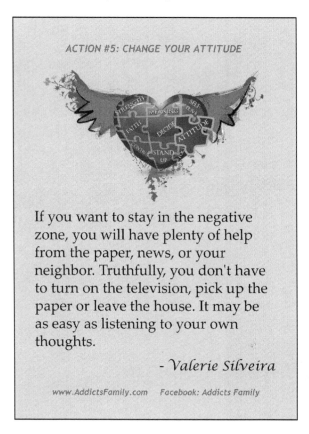

ACTION #5: CHANGE YOUR ATTITUDE

If you want to stay in the negative zone, you will have plenty of help from the paper, news, or your neighbor. Truthfully, you don't have to turn on the television, pick up the paper or leave the house. It may be as easy as listening to your own thoughts.

- *Valerie Silveira*

www.AddictsFamily.com   Facebook: Addicts Family

Negativity is everywhere, so it is easy to fall into the negative zone. You will have to make a serious effort to become a positive person and to stay positive. Nobody likes to be around a negative person, so make sure you are not around one every moment of every day.

Day Seventy-Eight

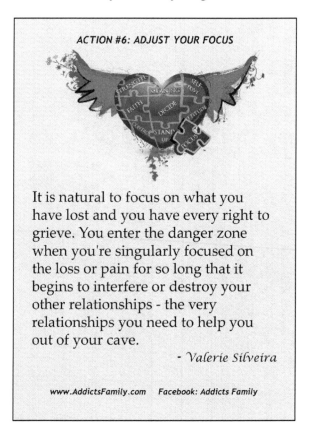

ACTION #6: ADJUST YOUR FOCUS

It is natural to focus on what you have lost and you have every right to grieve. You enter the danger zone when you're singularly focused on the loss or pain for so long that it begins to interfere or destroy your other relationships - the very relationships you need to help you out of your cave.

- *Valerie Silveira*

www.AddictsFamily.com   Facebook: Addicts Family

My daughter was quickly becoming the only person I was concerned about, including myself. I was very near giving up everyone and everything else, for the *chance* of "saving" her. Do not allow yourself to become stuck in the cave, alone, staring at the faded photo of your daughter or son.

Day Seventy-Nine

BATTLE YOUR CODEPENDENT ENABLER BEAST

If you are trying to save your children from themselves, you may want to consider retiring your cape. I put mine on so many times that it is ripped, stained, and frayed. It has been caught in doors, stuck in my underwear, and wrapped around my neck. At some point, it was just time to take it off.

- Valerie Silveira

www.AddictsFamily.com   facebook.com/Addict's Family

A part of you that remembers what your child was like before the drug Beast took over does not want you to remove the Supermom Cape. Another part still believes it is your responsibility to save them and does not think you can remove it. The part of you who understands you are not helping knows it is time.

Day Eighty

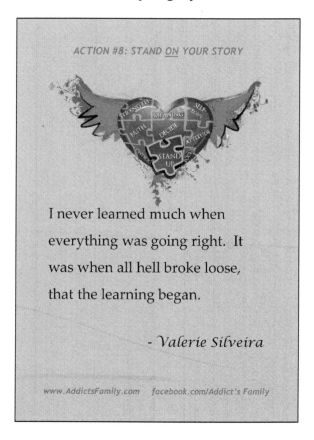

ACTION #8: STAND <u>ON</u> YOUR STORY

I never learned much when everything was going right. It was when all hell broke loose, that the learning began.

- *Valerie Silveira*

www.AddictsFamily.com   facebook.com/Addict's Family

Do not get me wrong; I love it when life is utter bliss. There are plenty of opportunities to give and share, and spread joy around when life is on an upward path. However, it is when all hell breaks loose that you will learn the most - if you are willing to learn.

Day Eighty-One

ACTION #9: MAKE MEANING FROM THE MADNESS

At this very moment, there is someone whose life you can touch; at least one person who will be better for having known you.

- *Valerie Silveira*

www.AddictsFamily.com   Facebook: Addicts Family

You are exhausted from trying to "help" your son or daughter. The thought of reaching out to anyone else, may not appeal to you, but there is something small that you can do or say that could influence another person for the rest of his or her life.

Day Eighty-Two

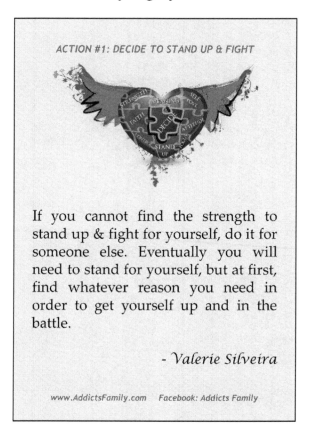

ACTION #1: DECIDE TO STAND UP & FIGHT

If you cannot find the strength to stand up & fight for yourself, do it for someone else. Eventually you will need to stand for yourself, but at first, find whatever reason you need in order to get yourself up and in the battle.

- *Valerie Silveira*

www.AddictsFamily.com   Facebook: Addicts Family

At first, you might not have the strength to stand up and fight for yourself. In the beginning, you may find it easier to stand up, for the sake of someone else. At first, I stood up to fight because of my son, who is not the addict. That is what it took for me to find the courage - I fought for him. Find your reason.

Day Eighty-Three

ACTION #2: GET ON YOUR SPIRITUAL ARMOR

Having faith is not a sign of weakness. When you are in a battle with a Beast, it is wise to bring your "big gun" - God!

- *Valerie Silveira*

www.AddictsFamily.com   facebook.com/Addict's Family

Often we feel as if we need to figure everything out, to have all of the answers. If we ask for help, if we turn to God, we are weak. Faith in a higher power takes courage, not weakness.

Day Eighty-Four

ACTION #3: PUT ON YOUR OXYGEN MASK

It is okay for you to be okay, when someone else isn't. Even your child.

- *Valerie Silveira*

www.AddictsFamily.com   Facebook: Addicts Family

Just because someone else is choosing not to be okay, does not make it wrong for you to choose to be okay. It is challenging when that someone is your son or daughter, but both of you self-destructing only compounds an already devastating situation. Choose to be okay – in fact, better than okay.

Day Eighty-Five

ACTION #4: BUILD YOUR CIRCLE OF STRENGTH

Make sure the right people
are in your Inner Circle.
Choose those who love you,
support you, and encourage
you to Stand Up & Fight.

- Valerie Silveira

www.AddictsFamily.com   facebook.com/Addicts Family

If you have the wrong people in your Inner Circle, you are setting
yourself up for disappointment and frustration. Your Inner Circle
should consist of those who support you the most in your battle.
They should also be people who will challenge you, or push you
to Stand Up and Fight.

Day Eighty-Six

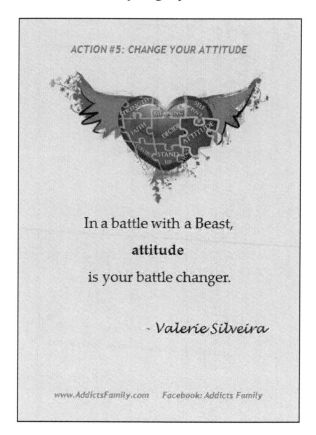

ACTION #5: CHANGE YOUR ATTITUDE

In a battle with a Beast,

attitude

is your battle changer.

- Valerie Silveira

www.AddictsFamily.com   Facebook: Addicts Family

Attitude might not be everything but is incredibly powerful. Having a good attitude will not magically change the direction of your son or daughter's life, but neither will a bad attitude. On the other hand, your attitude WILL affect the outcome of your battle.

Day Eighty-Seven

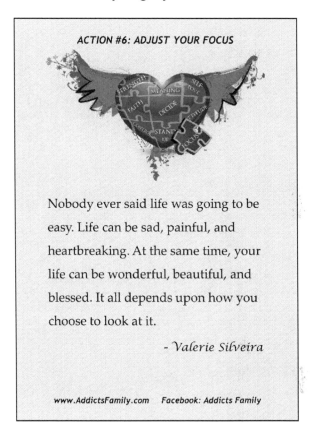

ACTION #6: ADJUST YOUR FOCUS

Nobody ever said life was going to be easy. Life can be sad, painful, and heartbreaking. At the same time, your life can be wonderful, beautiful, and blessed. It all depends upon how you choose to look at it.

- *Valerie Silveira*

www.AddictsFamily.com   Facebook: Addicts Family

The fact is that moms of addicts walk a very rough road, filled with anxiety, sadness, loneliness, heartbreak, fear, and so much more. Plenty of people go through situations as tough as yours, and worse. Among the devastation, you can find beauty, blessings, hope, and much more – if you choose to see it.

105

Day Eighty-Eight

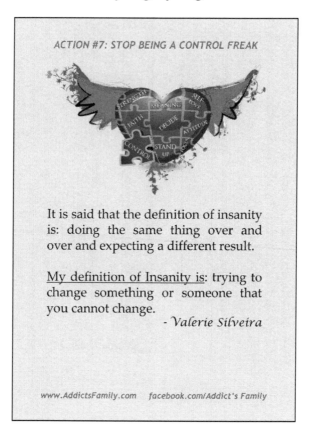

ACTION #7: STOP BEING A CONTROL FREAK

It is said that the definition of insanity is: doing the same thing over and over and expecting a different result.

My definition of Insanity is: trying to change something or someone that you cannot change.
- *Valerie Silveira*

www.AddictsFamily.com   facebook.com/Addict's Family

The real definition of insanity is trying to change something or someone you cannot change. You know the outcome of continuing the madness – more of the same, so stop. Start focusing on what you can control, what you can change.

Day Eighty-Nine

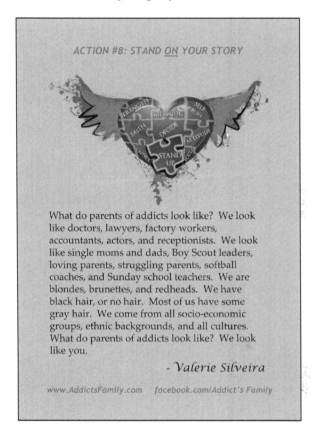

ACTION #8: STAND <u>ON</u> YOUR STORY

What do parents of addicts look like? We look like doctors, lawyers, factory workers, accountants, actors, and receptionists. We look like single moms and dads, Boy Scout leaders, loving parents, struggling parents, softball coaches, and Sunday school teachers. We are blondes, brunettes, and redheads. We have black hair, or no hair. Most of us have some gray hair. We come from all socio-economic groups, ethnic backgrounds, and all cultures. What do parents of addicts look like? We look like you.

- Valerie Silveira

www.AddictsFamily.com   facebook.com/Addict's Family

Hold your head high and be confident that you are not alone. Sadly, there are more families affected by addiction than you might realize. It happens to excellent mothers, with children who grew up in good homes. If you feel judged, remember that it can and does happen to anyone.

Day Ninety

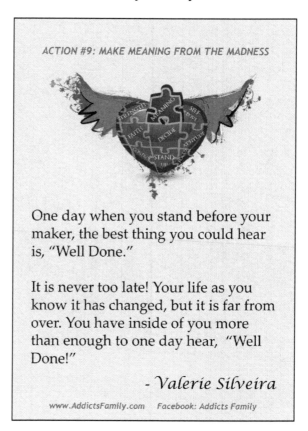

ACTION #9: MAKE MEANING FROM THE MADNESS

One day when you stand before your maker, the best thing you could hear is, "Well Done."

It is never too late! Your life as you know it has changed, but it is far from over. You have inside of you more than enough to one day hear, "Well Done!"

- Valerie Silveira

www.AddictsFamily.com   Facebook: Addicts Family

For the longest time, I didn't think my life would get any better, or that I could make a difference in the world. That was before I made my decision to stand up and fight. It is not over for you, no matter how you feel at this moment. Someone is waiting for you to make meaning– there is still time to hear, "Well Done."

Keeping the Pieces Together

There are many things you can do to continue battling your Beast, to help you put the pieces back together, and to keep them together.

- Read, "Still Standing After All the Tears."
- Go through the "Still Standing After All the Tears Workbook."
- Get a copy of "Misery, You Don't Get My Company."
- Get the e-book version of this book for beautiful color versions of the quotes, to access on your Smartphone, Kindle, iPad, or another device.
- Visit: www.ValerieSilveira.com:
    - Read all of the information.
    - Use the free tools.
    - Sign up to get the latest news & weekly inspiration.
    - Watch for more guidance and support tools.
    - Start a support group, using the Workbook.
- Follow Valerie on Facebook.

- Come to a Still Standing LIVE event.

- Start living the Nine Actions to Battle Your Beast.

- Let us know what other tools, or support topics you want to see in the future.

Stay Connected with Valerie

www.ValerieSilveira.com

STILL STANDING

AFTER ALL THE TEARS

PUTTING BACK THE PIECES AFTER ALL HELL BREAKS LOOSE

NINE ACTIONS TO BATTLE YOUR BEAST

Valerie Silveira

STILL STANDING
AFTER ALL THE TEARS

Nine Actions to Battle Your Beast

WORKBOOK

Valerie Silveira

About the Author

Valerie Silveira, Author of the **Award-Winning** Book, *"Still Standing After All the Tears: Putting Back the Pieces After All Hell Breaks Loose"* and Creator of the Nine Actions to Battle Your Beast. She is an author of two other books, a speaker, mentor, coach, and consultant.

In 2004, Valerie's eighteen-year-old daughter was shot by her ex-boyfriend. Over the next decade, Jordan's* life spun out of control and as a result, Valerie's spiraled into darkness. She would face the heartbreaking reality that Jordan was a heroin addict and the painful truth that she is powerless to save her from her Beast.

With a heart shattered into a million pieces, a broken family, health issues, financial hardship and depression, Valerie was giving up hope of ever being happy again. At a very dark time in her life, she found a shred of hope, and a tiny bit of courage, and made a decision that probably saved her life – she decided to Stand Up & Fight. *"Still Standing After All the Tears"* takes you on a journey through the agony and hopelessness of losing her child over and over again to drug addiction, and into the Actions, Valerie used to battle her own Codependent Enabler Beast. Moms all over the United States, Canada, the U.K., Australia, and New Zealand are following the Nine Actions and learning how to Stand Up & Fight.

Although Valerie was painfully aware of the possibility of Jordan dying from an overdose, nothing could have prepared her for that knock on the door, August 28, 2016. Her daughter, Jamie, (whom she had called Jordan), was murdered. The nightmare her family lived through in 2004, had returned. Only this time, Jamie didn't make it.

Through the devastation of losing Jamie, of losing hope of her recovery, Valerie has fought to regain her courage, to stand up again, and to continue her mission of helping moms and others. She is living proof that it is possible, even in your darkest hours, to Stand Up & Fight.

Valerie has had a diverse career in finance, business operations, consulting, training and speaking. None of her business challenges came even close to that of trying helplessly to save her daughter. She uses her professional experience and her two rides on what she calls the Roller Coaster From Hell, to help others put the pieces of their life back together. Valerie has an incredibly relatable style, and her sense of humor shows through the pain. The book and the Actions are important not only for families of addicts but for anyone struggling to move through or past a traumatic life situation.

*Until Jamie's death, Valerie chose to call her daughter "Jordan" out of respect for her story.

Stay Connected with Valerie:

www.ValerieSilveira.com